JUST A LITTLE BIT MORE
THE HEART OF A MENTOR

Accounts of Cross-cultural Mentoring
and the Lessons they Hold

DR. BOB ABRAMSON

WORKBOOK

Alphabet Resources

Just a Little Bit More - WORKBOOK
Published by Alphabet Resources, Inc.
365 Stonehenge Drive
Phillipsburg, NJ 08865
1-908-213-2997
info@mentoringministry.com

Cover design by Ryan Stacey

10 digit ISBN 0-9843443-1-4
13 digit ISBN 978-0-9843443-1-4

Contact Dr. Abramson by visiting
www.mentoringministry.com

The workbook is a study aid to be used with Dr. Abramson's book, "JUST A LITTLE BIT MORE." It is not intended or designed to stand alone. The questions and exercises contained in this workbook require the reader to study and work with the book.

CONTENTS OF THE WORKBOOK

Introduction

"A great leader is not a man who does great things, but a man who gets others to do great things." (President Ronald Reagan)

Read the Introduction in our text. Take time to reflect on what you have read. Think about the following statements that represent principles related to issues every leader faces and must understand. Answer the questions provided with each principle below. Be as honest and transparent as you can. If possible, discuss your answers within a group.

Principles for Discussion

Principle 1 | **Do not expect convenience. Mentoring has its price. It will cost you.**

a. What would you expect would be most difficult about mentoring people?

_____

_____

_____

b. What would you expect to give up when becoming somebody's mentor?

_____

_____

_____

Principle 2 | **Mentoring has its rewards. It will cost you, but bless you far beyond the cost.**

a. What kinds of blessings would you desire for yourself from the mentoring process?

_____

_____

_____

b. What kinds of blessings would you want most for those you mentor, as a result of the mentoring process?

_____

_____

_____

_____

Summary Mentoring Definitions

Summary definitions of mentoring are provided at the end of the Introduction and after each chapter. These definitions come from combining the mentoring principles found throughout the text. Each of these mentoring principles, and their chapter-ending summaries, will represent different facets of the mentoring process. At the conclusion of Chapter 10, a "Final, Concise Definition of Mentoring" will be given. This has been pulled together from these chapter-ending summaries. Now, consider our first summary definition of mentoring, found at end of the Introduction.

> **Mentoring is the intentional process of loving and nurturing the people God assigns us along the way to our destinies. It is a costly exercise in profound personal sacrifice, leading to growth and change. It is an open door to divinely inspired relationships.**

Give any comments or criticisms you have of the above summary definition.

_____

_____

_____

_____

Before you begin the first chapter, I would like you to compile two lists, which I have set out for you. Please take your time and think them through. Then pencil in your answers. As you go through the book, I invite you to refer to your lists and reflect on what the book is saying to you about what you have written. Change the lists as you go through the chapters. When you come to the end of the book, I encourage you to compile a final list. Compare it to your first list, and any subsequent changes you have made. You might be surprised at how some of your thoughts will have changed. You will have a clearer understanding of mentoring. Beyond that, you will have a better understanding of the awesome opportunities God will give you to learn, grow, and understand, as you teach, empower and help others to mature in Christ. Here are the lists.

List five conditions you would require in order to commit to mentoring someone.

1.

2.

3.

4.

5.

List five conditions that would stop you from committing to mentoring someone.

1.

2.

3.

4.

5.

Chapter 1 - An Unlikely Disciple

Read Chapter 1. Reflect on what you have read. When you have done so, answer the questions provided with each principle below. As always, be as honest and transparent as you can. If possible, discuss your answers within a group.

Principles for Discussion

Principle 1 | **Take a risk. Open your heart!**

a. What does it mean to open your heart? Explain.

_____

_____

_____

_____

b. What risk would you fear the most about opening your heart to a potential disciple?

_____

_____

_____

_____

Principle 2 | **Mentoring will cause you to go beyond yourself. Your disciples will take you to places in Christ that you have never visited before.**

a. Describe two key challenges you would expect to face in the mentoring process.

Key Challenge #1

_____

_____

_____

Key Challenge #2

_____

_____

_____

b. Where spiritually would you hope the mentoring process would take you, that you have not yet gone?

_____

_____

_____

_____

| Principle 3 | **Assume little and you will learn much.**

a. What assumptions, right or wrong, do most people make about the mentoring process?

_____

_____

_____

_____

b. What do you think would be the hardest thing to learn within the mentoring process?

_____

_____

_____

_____

| Principle 4 | **God will be the deciding factor in the mentoring process.**

a. What makes God the deciding factor?

_____

_____

_____

_____

b. If God is the deciding factor, what part is left to us?

_____

_____

_____

_____

Principle 5 | It is not so much about how you do it, but who you are when you do it.

a. What do you think God looks for most when He selects a person to mentor another? Make a list.

1.	4.
2.	5.
3.	6.

b. What do you think God looks for most when He selects a person to be mentored? Make a list.

1.	4.
2.	5.
3.	6.

Summary Mentoring Definition - Chapter 1

Mentoring is a carefully learned, relearned, and skillfully practiced craft. It begins with a season of planting into the good soil of lives that bud, blossom, bloom and grow. It is a steadfast dedication to a heartfelt, committed, ever-growing one-on-one relationship.

Mentoring is commitment to a special relationship of grace, in which communication, communion, participation and partnership all contribute to a process of imitation by those we mentor. This results in growth and maturity in Christ.

Give any comments or criticisms you have of the summary definition, above.

_____

_____

_____

_____

_____

_____

Compare your comments or criticisms, to those from the Introduction. Record any strong thoughts or troubling issues you have arrived at.

_____

_____

_____

_____

_____

_____

_____

_____

Chapter 2 - Expect the Unexpected!

Read Chapter 2. Reflect on what you have read. When you have done so, answer the questions provided with each principle below. As always, be as honest and transparent as you can. If possible, discuss your answers within a group.

Principles for Discussion

Principle 1 | **Take hold of your character and invest it with great care and caution.**

a. What does it mean to invest something?

_____

_____

_____

_____

_____

b. When you invest your character, what are you really investing?

_____

_____

_____

_____

_____

Principle 2 | **Understand the value of the people God gives you to love and care for.**

a. What determines somebody's value to you?

_____

_____

_____

_____

b. Are there varying degrees of value that you should put on people? Explain your answer.

_____

_____

_____

_____

_____

| Principle 3 | Expect the unexpected. It will surely happen.

a. Life is full of surprises. What should be your first reaction to a surprise in ministry?

_____

_____

_____

_____

_____

b. How should you make decisions when confronted with surprises? Describe the process.

_____

_____

_____

_____

_____

| Principle 4 | The goal of discipline is that those you discipline will be better for the experience and not likely to stumble as easily again.

a. In what ways should they be better for the experience?

_____

_____

_____

_____

_____

b. What would you try to achieve that would help them (1) recognize and (2) change because of the experience?

_____

_____

_____

_____

_____

| Principle 5 | **When your disciples let you down, turn to God and cry, "Grace!" He will give it to you.** |

a. What attitudes will you need to guard against when you are disappointed by people?

_____

_____

_____

_____

_____

b. What will grace give you in these moments when your disciples let you down?

_____

_____

_____

_____

_____

| Principle 6 | **When you let grace have room in your heart, it will turn a devastating circumstance into a teachable moment and a terrific victory.** |

a. What does it mean to "give grace room in your heart?"

_____

_____

_____

_____

b. Name three typical attitudes that would get in the way of giving it room. Give a Scriptural answer to each that will help you to welcome grace into your heart in these times.

1. _____
_____
_____

2. _____
_____
_____

3. _____
_____
_____

Principle 7 **When the unexpected happens, wrap yourself in God's Word, His character and His love. They will see you through.**

a. Think about the idea of wrapping yourself in something. Put Principle 7 into your own words.

_____
_____
_____
_____
_____

b. How would you wrap yourself in God's Word, His character and His love? Be specific - no clichés.

_____
_____
_____
_____
_____

| Principle 8 | Even when you fail in what you have tried, you can become a success in who you have become. |

a. What would allow you to you call yourself a success if your mentoring efforts seem to fail?

_____

_____

_____

_____

_____

b. Does your success depend on the successes of those you mentor? Why? ...Why not?

_____

_____

_____

_____

_____

Summary Mentoring Definition - Chapter 2

Mentoring is being as much like Jesus as you can possibly be, so they can become as much like Jesus as they can possibly be. It is done through the application of God's Word, the display of His character and the outworking of His love in you, instilling the same in others. This can be understood as the process of intentional Christ-like behavior for the explicit purpose of affecting others with His grace.

Give any comments or criticisms you have of the summary definition, above.

_____

_____

_____

_____

_____

_____
_____
_____
_____

Compare your comments or criticisms to those from the Introduction and Chapter 1. As before, record any strong thoughts or troubling issues you have arrived at.

_____
_____
_____
_____
_____
_____
_____
_____
_____

Chapter 3 - They will Catch your Heart!

Read Chapter 3. Reflect on what you have read. When you have done so, answer the questions provided for each principle below. As always, be as honest and transparent as you can. If possible, discuss your answers within a group.

Principles for Discussion

Principle 1 | **Affirm them with truth and love. The truth will set them free and the love will keep them secure.**

a. Discuss the kinds of words you would use to affirm the people you mentor.

_____
_____
_____
_____
_____

b. How would you approach one of your disciples who was discouraged and acting out a personal pity party?

_____
_____
_____
_____
_____
_____

Principle 2 | **If they can catch your heart, it will transform their lives.**

a. Examine your heart in the condition it is in today. What could others catch from you that would transform them in a positive way?

_____
_____

_____
_____
_____
_____

b. What barriers would commonly stop others from catching what is in your heart?

_____
_____
_____
_____

| Principle 3 | **When the season of mentoring is finished, give them back to God and believe the best for them.** |

a. What emotions might a mentor experience that could hinder letting go of people when the time comes to do so?

_____
_____
_____
_____

b. Aside from a date on a calendar, how can we typically know that a season of mentoring is finished?

_____
_____
_____
_____

| Principle 4 | **Focus on their growth, not their usefulness.** |

a. It is always tempting to use the people we mentor for our advantage. They are typically ready and willing to serve us in any way we ask. What temptations might you face as a mentor that might be helpful to the tasks at hand, but would hinder your disciples from catching your heart?

18

b. Give three milestones you would like to establish for your disciples that have nothing to do with their usefulness, but would be a valid measure of their growth.

Milestone #1

Milestone #2

Milestone #3

Principle 5 **If they catch your heart, they will grow into their destinies.**

a. Why would your disciples have to "grow" into their destinies? Explain the connection between them catching what is in your heart and their growth. Where would the growth take place?

b. Can they catch your heart without you catching theirs? Explain.

Summary Mentoring Definition - Chapter 3

Mentoring is the act of preparing others for life's tough decisions. It is equipping them to be ready for the inevitable choices they will face. Mentoring is involving our hearts with the hearts of those we mentor. In doing so, we encourage them to reach for their dreams and embrace their destinies.

Give any comments or criticisms you have of the summary definition, above.

_____

_____

_____

_____

_____

_____

_____

_____

Compare your comments or criticisms to those from the Introduction and Chapters 1-2. As before, record any strong thoughts or troubling issues you have arrived at.

_____

_____

_____

_____

_____

_____

_____

_____

_____

Chapter 4 - It takes a Father to make a Son.

There comes a special time in every mentor's life when God sends a singularly exceptional person to be mentored. Pray that in the appropriate season, you recognize this person. It can be a life-changing experience for both of you. Read Chapter 4. Reflect on what you have read. Answer the questions provided with each principle below. As always, be as honest and transparent as you can. If you can, discuss your answers within a group.

Principles for Discussion

Principle 1 | **You will have your disappointments. Remember, disappointment is an opportunity for another appointment - an appointment with God.**

a. What role has disappointment played in your growth as a Christian and a leader?

_____

_____

_____

_____

_____

_____

b. When you experienced disappointment, what did somebody do or say that influenced your ability to advance to your next opportunity? Did you ever think of it as another appointment with God?

_____

_____

_____

_____

_____

_____

_____

Principle 2 — **Show them the heart of God and the principles of His Word. You will teach them all they need to know.**

a. Where would you direct people in order for them to learn the heart of God? List at least three things. Explain why, for each.

1. _____

2. _____

3. _____

4. _____

b. What would you pick to be the three most important principles of God's Word you could teach your disciples? Why?

1. _____

2. _____

3. _____

Principle 3 — **Mentoring is the process of instilling a desire for imitation in your disciples - imitation of Someone far greater than you.**

a. What would be some good methods to use to get someone you are mentoring to imitate Christ?

_____

_____

_____

_____

_____

_____

b. What is there about ministry that is often and easily imitated but not necessarily good?

_____

_____

_____

_____

_____

Principle 4 | **Look for the destiny in them and you will find the destiny in yourself.**

a. What is destiny? Define it in your own words. Why is it important?

_____

_____

_____

_____

_____

_____

b. Why would you find destiny in yourself if you were looking for destiny in others?

_____

_____

_____

_____

_____

_____

Principle 5 | **There is value in diversity. God gives it life. We nourish it and give it room to express itself and grow.**

a. What is the value of the having diversity of thought and personality in those you mentor?

_____

_____

_____

_____

_____

b. Give at least two ways you can give diversity room for expression that create opportunities for growth in the mentoring process.
   1.
   _____
   _____
   2.
   _____
   _____
   3.
   _____
   _____

Principle 6 | **Their ways may be different, but may not be wrong. Give them room to be who they are. Keep your mind as open as you have kept your heart.**

a. What determines whether someone's ways are right or wrong?
   _____
   _____
   _____

b. What keeps our minds from being open to differences in people?
   _____
   _____
   _____

Principle 7 | **Mentoring is like a swim in deep waters. When the waters get deep and seem dangerous... pray, believe God and keep swimming. You will make it to the other side.**

a. Swimming takes more than faith. It is an acquired skill. What practical skills can you help others acquire that will help them to keep on going when the going gets tough?
   _____
   _____
   _____

b. Swimming to the other side in tough times is not just for those you mentor. You will have occasion to do the same. What is there about mentoring that can become like deep and dangerous waters?

| Principle 8 | **Give them your best. Believe God for the rest. It will come to pass. You will bear fruit and your fruit will remain.** |

a. Define what your best would be in any mentoring situation.

b. Your best is sometimes found in your mentoring failures. When might this happen and what might the failure be?

| Principle 9 | **When your disciples become disciple makers, you have evidence that your spiritual sons have become like their father.** |

a. What does it mean for a son to be like his father?

---

b. What would it mean for you to have spiritual sons and daughters?

Summary Mentoring Definition - Chapter 4

Mentoring is the father-like process of building character and commitment. It is an experience in which disappointments can open doors to new dreams and the fulfillment of God's best. Teach them to expect the unexpected, and welcome it.

Mentoring is the act of coaching, in which we point the way for others to imitate and embrace the same lifestyle we have imitated and embraced - not ours, but the lifestyle of Christ. In this process, we give our disciples room to be themselves, freedom to do things their way and opportunities to discover the value of our ways.

Give any comments or criticisms you have of the summary definition, above.

Compare your comments or criticisms to those from the Introduction and Chapters 1-3. As before, record strong thoughts or troubling issues you have arrived at.

_____
_____
_____
_____
_____
_____
_____
_____

Chapter 5 - Landmarks in their Lives

A landmark is a clearly recognizable sign of a significant historical event, or an achievement worth noting, taking place at a particular point in time. Have you ever considered what landmarks you should be able to see in your disciples, long after they have gone beyond the times when you actively influenced them? What will their lives say?

Read Chapter 5. Reflect on what you have read. Then, review the five landmarks given in this chapter.

1. Continuing Fruitfulness - After they have left you
2. Reports of their Steadfast Character and Christ-likeness
3. Genuine Humility in the Conduct of their Lives
4. Indisputable Signs of the Lordship of Christ
5. Compelling, Unwavering Service to God

Answer the questions provided with each principle below. As always, be honest and transparent. If possible, discuss your answers within a group.

Principles for Discussion

| Principle 1 | As you recognize God working in them, challenge them to respond. They will go places in God only He could have made possible. |

a. What are the most important challenges you could offer them?

_____

_____

_____

_____

_____

_____

_____

b. When and how will you know you are to release them from your leadership and influence?

_____

_____

_____

_____

_____

c. What will you see in them that will tell you it is time?

_____

_____

_____

_____

_____

| Principle 2 | **If you do your best, they will do theirs.**

a. How would you define your best? Give two distinct approaches to answering this question.

   1. _____

_____

_____

_____

   2. _____

_____

_____

_____

b. What can you expect to be their best?

_____

_____

_____

_____

Principle 3 Genuine humility is a spiritual response to an understanding of self, in light of Christ. God is God and we are not.

a. What is a spiritual response?

_____

_____

_____

_____

b. What are the ingredients necessary to give a person an understanding of self?

_____

_____

_____

_____

c. Explain your understanding of what is meant by the term "self." Talk about both the good and bad meanings of this term.

_____

_____

_____

_____

Principle 4 Pray for them only after you have found it in your heart to love them.

a. What is the difference between praying for someone without love and compassion and praying for them with genuine, heartfelt feelings of love and compassion?

_____

_____

_____

_____

b. How does compassionate, loving praying affect you? What about those you pray for? Does it make any difference to God, or will He respond regardless of how you pray?

_____

_____

_____

_____

_____

| Principle 5 | **Make Him Lord and watch Him perform His Word.**

a. Can Jesus be your Savior but not your Lord? If this were the case, how would it affect your ability to influence those you mentor or lead?

_____

_____

_____

_____

_____

b. If Jesus is Savior but not their Lord to those you mentor or lead, how will it affect your ability to influence them (and your prayers for them)?

_____

_____

_____

_____

_____

c. You cannot control what others choose, but let's talk about you. Consider the following three questions and be honest with yourself.

1. Have you accepted Jesus as your personal Savior? If so, briefly describe your experience of salvation, in the manner you would use it to testify to others.

_____

_____

_____

_____

2. Can you say you have an intimate, personal relationship with Him every hour of every day? What about in all things? Are there any areas of your life you purposely exclude Him?

---

3. On a scale of 1-100 (100 signifying complete), how would you rate your submission to Jesus as your Lord? Today could be a landmark if you resolve in your heart to improve the quality of your life in Christ. Will you do it? How?

| Principle 6 | **A Landmark is a clearly recognizable sign of a significant historical event, or an achievement worth noting, taking place at a particular point in time. Life's landmarks provide us with evidence for our faith to stand strong.** |

a. What landmark would you most like to reach in your immediate future?

---

b. Describe a landmark of yours (now or in the future) that you would most like people to remember, from which they could take encouragement for their own lives.

_____

_____

_____

_____

_____

_____

Summary Mentoring Definition - Chapter 5

Mentoring is your best service to others to insure they will embrace and fulfill their destinies. Mentoring challenges all involved with new ideas and examples. As a result, everyone finds themselves rethinking ideas they previously believed to be valid. This leads to what are often tough choices and sometimes even tougher changes.

Give any comments or criticisms you have of the summary definition, above.

_____

_____

_____

_____

_____

_____

Compare your comments or criticisms to those from the Introduction and Chapters 1-4. As before, record strong thoughts or troubling issues you have arrived at.

_____

_____

_____

_____

_____
_____
_____
_____
_____

At the end of the Introduction (page 5) you compiled two lists. Reconsider what you wrote and where necessary, rewrite them based on what has challenged you so far. Keep your original lists for later comparison. Here again are the lists.

List five conditions you would require in order to commit to mentoring someone.

1. _____

2. _____

3. _____

4. _____

5. _____

List five conditions that would stop you from committing to mentoring someone.

1. _____

2. _____

3. _____

4.

5.

Chapter 6 - How will you Answer the Rain?

The challenge to us, as mentors, is to walk through our own disappointments in ways that demonstrate faith and perseverance to others. If we are trusting and faithful in times when trouble rains down on us, and we refuse to give in to the circumstances, those watching will be apprehended by what they see. They will gain the inspiration and tools to go successfully beyond their own inevitable moments of stress, disappointment and apparent failure. Read Chapter 6. Reflect on what you have read. Answer the questions provided with each principle below. As always, be as honest and transparent as you can. If possible, discuss your answers within a group.

Principles for Discussion

Principle 1 | **When you are in the grip of your trouble, let yourself be gripped by His grace. God has the stronger hand. He will always prevail.**

a. Why is God's grip on you always more powerful than the grip your trouble may have? Back up what you say with two Scriptures that make a deep impression on your heart.

_____

_____

Scripture #1

_____

Scripture #2

_____

b. List three of God's promises you routinely claim in your prayers that will help you when trouble strikes. If you do not have them, take the time to find them in His Word.

Promise #1

_____

_____

Promise #2

Promise #3

c. Explain what you think it means to be gripped by His grace. Provide a Scriptural basis.

Principle 2 | **If you choose to live in His grip before your trouble, you will stay safely in it during your trouble. When the trouble has passed, you will still be in His grip, and His fingerprints will be on your victory... and on you.**

a. Briefly list three practical steps you can take to live in His grip (to make it a lifestyle).

1.

2.

3.

b. List three typical barriers believers face trying to living a lifestyle in the grip of God.

Barrier #1

Barrier #2

Barrier #3

c. In addition to prayer, what are the answers to overcoming these barriers?

Answer to Barrier #1

_____

_____

Answer to Barrier #2

_____

_____

Answer to Barrier #3

_____

_____

| Principle 3 | Faith is not about results. It is about unwavering trust in God, regardless of any apparent circumstances or outcomes. |

a. What is there in your life that consistently challenges the exercise of your faith?

_____

_____

_____

_____

b. Do you find yourself having anxiety or fear when these challenges come? What should you do to conquer these things?

_____

_____

_____

| Principle 4 | Faith never gives in, never gives up, and never gives out! |

a. What do you think is the driving force behind personal perseverance?

_____

_____

_____

_____

b. Name three things you could do to strengthen your own ability to persevere in anything you might face.

1. _____

2. _____

3. _____

_____

_____

_____

| Principle 5 | If you fill their bowls, faith will fill yours.

a. What can you begin to do that you are not already doing, within your present daily routine, to fill the bowls of others?

_____

_____

_____

_____

_____

b. Explain the a connection between giving of yourself to others and having your needs met. List three Scriptures to back up your argument.

_____

_____

_____

_____

Scripture #1 _____

Scripture #2 _____

Scripture #3 _____

_____

Principle 6 Tough times never last. Tough people do. Answer your rainstorms with faith.

a. What can believers do to become spiritually toughened, so the trials and tests of life do not overwhelm them?

_____

_____

_____

_____

b. What three Scriptures would you personally apply when working toward becoming spiritually toughened, so you could answer your rainstorms with faith?

Scripture #1

_____

Scripture #2

_____

Scripture #3

_____

Principle 7 Faith works in the sunshine just as well as in the rain.

a. What carnal temptations do believers typically fall into when significant opportunities present themselves?

_____

_____

_____

_____

b. If a person relies on "self" in the "good times," why will it be difficult to turn to God in the "hard times?"

_____

_____

_____

_____

_____

c. If a person habitually relies on God in the "good times," why will it be easier to turn to Him in the "hard times?"

_____

_____

_____

_____

Summary Mentoring Definition - Chapter 6

Mentoring is the sum of three parts - (1) teaching what they need to know, (2) helping them practice what they have been taught, and (3) imparting to them the faith to grow and walk in victory. Always give preference to the third part - impartation of faith.

Mentoring is always to be a display of the mentor's faith, which God uses to increase the strength of the belief systems of those who are watching, listening and learning.

Give any comments or criticisms you have of the summary definition, above.

_____

_____

_____

_____

_____

_____

_____

_____

Compare your comments or criticisms to those from the Introduction and Chapters 1-5. As before, record strong thoughts or troubling issues you have.

Chapter 7 - Inconvenient Love

(1 John 2:9-11 NKJV) "He who says he is in the light, and hates his brother, is in darkness until now. {10} He who loves his brother abides in the light, and there is no cause for stumbling in him. {11} But he who hates his brother is in darkness and walks in darkness, and does not know where he is going, because the darkness has blinded his eyes."

There will be times when you find yourself mentoring people you have neither chosen nor desired to have as disciples. They will be those who God chooses for you, not the ones you choose for yourself. He will bring them across your path and ask you to commit yourself to them. You may feel no affinity for them. Your feelings may be quite the opposite. You may even feel distaste and the desire to distance yourself from them. However, these are points in time when there is kingdom business to be done. In these times, you will have to look deeply within yourself. God will ask you to surrender your feelings, to crucify them and embrace your opportunity to be compassionate, merciful and yes, even loving. You will have to see them through the eyes of Christ, and not your own eyes. Regardless of what your mind, will and emotions tell you, you will be confronted with this challenge. The Holy Spirit will ask if you will freely embrace them as Christ would. Will you go beyond what your feelings want or do not want? Will you love those who seem to you to be so unlovely?

Read Chapter 7. Reflect on what you have read. Answer the questions provided with each principle below. As always, be as honest and transparent as you can. If possible, discuss your answers in a group.

Principles for Discussion

Principle 1 | **Loving the unlovely requires complete surrender to grace.**

a. What strong personal prejudices or opinions hinder people from a heart of grace toward certain other people? What does God think of them? Are you in any way prejudiced? Be honest with yourself as you answer.

45

JUST A LITTLE BIT MORE

_____

_____

_____

_____

_____

b. If you have any prejudices (and most of us do), what could you do to change or remove them?

_____

_____

_____

_____

_____

| Principle 2 | **One-on-one mentoring encounters are divine appointments - never for two, always for three.** |

a. What signals should you be alert to, so you will recognize when God is arranging a significant mentoring encounter for you? Answering this will take some thought.

_____

_____

_____

_____

_____

b. Name three questions you typically should ask yourself, as you determine your course of action when considering a new person to mentor.

1. _____

2. _____

3. _____

Principle 3 | **Is it only a religious charade in a religious parade?**

a. What can you do to check your heart to be sure you are not being a hypocrite with your words or actions?

_____

_____

_____

_____

b. What should be your immediate response if you find yourself performing a religious charade? (This also should take some considered thought.) Try to sort this out into some sort of progressive response that takes you to a new place in Christ.

_____

_____

_____

_____

Progressive Response:

1. _____

2. _____

3. _____

4. _____

Principle 4 | **One of the great tests of leadership is whether we will reject the temptation to judge and make the choice to embrace the demands of love.**

a. List the two things are you always (habitually) too quick to judge people about. What is the Bible's answer to these two sins? (Yes, they are sins.)

1. _____

_____

Biblical Answer

2.

Biblical Answer

b. In addition to what you already have written, is there anything else you could do to be more like Jesus in the way you view others?

| Principle 5 | **Never make the mistake of trying to write the guest list to the communion table yourself.** |

a. How well do you submit your personal choices about people you encounter to the Spirit of God for direction, correction and enlightenment? How could you make this a more habitual response to your encounters with them?

b. How aware are you of your own shortcomings when you begin to judge others?

Do not be surprised if this has been your most challenging chapter in the book. Having God's kind of love always seems to be a challenge. However, God continually encourages us to have the heart and mind of Christ. We can progressively become more like Jesus every day, in every way. It takes a holy discontent with the way we are today and a willingness to change for tomorrow. Remember, your yesterdays are not qualified to determine your tomorrows. Yesterday is under the blood of Christ. God has great tomorrows waiting for you. What you do today is what is important. It will determine who you are tomorrow.

Your yesterdays are not qualified to determine your tomorrows.

Summary Mentoring Definition - Chapter 7

Mentoring is the intentional application of contagious, Christ-like compassion. It is a deliberate course of action, in which we become God's gifts to each other. In this exchange, we open the door to communion with Christ through the exercise of our love, no matter how inconvenient it may be.

Give any comments or criticisms you have of the summary definition, above.

_____
_____
_____
_____
_____
_____
_____
_____

Compare your comments or criticisms to those from the Introduction and Chapters 1-6. As before, record any strong thoughts or troubling issues you have.

Chapter 8 - A Mentor's Guide to Survival

How will you handle the disappointments that inevitably come your way? What will you do when you encounter the pitfalls that await you in your service to the Lord? Read Chapter 8. Reflect on what you have read. Answer the questions provided with each principle below. As always, be as honest and transparent as you can. If possible, discuss your answers in a group.

Principles for Discussion

Principle 1 | **Only the people we mentor can break down their own barriers to growth.**

a. Are there areas of others' lives that you typically are too quick to try to manage, when God wants them to take responsibility for themselves? Identify three of these. Then give the biblical principle that can change your wanting to do too much micro-management.

Area #1
_____

Principle for change
_____
_____

Area #2
_____

Principle for change
_____
_____

Area #3
_____

Principle for change
_____
_____

b. What is the primary attitude you need to change so others take responsibility for themselves?

_____

_____

_____

_____

| Principle 2 | **Spending yourself where there is no fruitfulness will keep you from being effective where and when it counts.** |

a. List at least three things you can observe that will help determine the potential for fruitfulness in the lives of those you mentor.

1. _____

2. _____

3. _____

_____

b. What would be the primary signal that you should terminate your mentoring efforts with someone?

_____

_____

_____

_____

| Principle 3 | **Patience is a great challenge for newly emerging leadership.** |

a. What do people do that typically tries your patience?

_____

_____

_____

b. What lesson would you teach from what you just identified?

_____

_____

_____

_____

| **Principle 4** | **Expect the unexpected. It will surely happen. There are no surprises in heaven. God is in control.** |

a. How do you typically react to surprises that challenge the status-quo of your ministry (or your life)?

_____

_____

_____

_____

b. Are you comfortable leaving room for variations in your plans and programs? If not, why? If so, how do you usually react when the unexpected happens?

_____

_____

_____

_____

| **Principle 5** | **A good leader is a reachable leader, just as a good disciple is a reachable disciple. Keep on reaching. Keep on teaching.** |

a. Identify what you think are correct or incorrect teachings about a leader's position, relative to those who are his or her followers.

Correct: _____

_____

Incorrect: _____

_____

b. Has anything you read in this chapter challenge or offend you because of what you have been taught? If so, what is it and what will you do?

_____

_____

_____

_____

_____

Summary Mentoring Definition - Chapter 8

Mentoring is a measured process or course of action in which people are challenged to embrace your efforts and show fruit in theirs. It is the business of facilitating another person's development and self-discovery.

Give any comments or criticisms you have of the summary definition, above.

_____

_____

_____

_____

_____

_____

_____

Compare your comments or criticisms to those from the Introduction and Chapters 1-7. As before, record strong thoughts or troubling issues you have arrived at.

_____

_____

_____

_____

_____

_____

_____

Chapter 9 - Transitions

Understanding the dynamics of seasons and what happens when they end will help you go forward, better able to handle the next season. You will become more proficient in your servant-leadership to those you touch. Read Chapter 9. Reflect on what you have read. Answer the questions provided with each principle below. As always, be as honest and transparent as you can. If possible, discuss your answers in a group.

Principles for Discussion

Principle 1 Someone's destiny is always waiting on the other side of your obedience.

a. What area of obedience in ministry do you struggle with most? Why?

_____

_____

_____

_____

b. When do your emotions cloud your judgment and negatively sway your decisions?

_____

_____

_____

_____

Principle 2 Never question obedience to the voice of God. He always knows best for all concerned.

a. What can you do to assure yourself that you have heard the voice of God?

_____

_____

_____

b. When are you unsure about whether you heard the voice of God, or perhaps confused it with someone else's voice? What can you do to try to resolve this?

_____

_____

_____

_____

_____

| Principle 3 | It is important to count the cost of your decisions, as you serve God. However, when the cost seems overwhelming, stop counting the cost and start counting it all joy. |

a. What do you typically think of when you think of the cost of giving yourself to ministry?

_____

_____

_____

_____

_____

b. Identify the thresholds (lines beyond which you might struggle to cross) for you when the cost becomes a problem for your obedience. Everyone has thresholds. Name and elaborate on at least three of them. Then identify Scripture that will encourage you to cross these thresholds.

1. _____

_____

Scripture _____

2. _____

_____

Scripture _____

3.

Scripture

Principle 4 | **We flourish most when our faith is forced to flourish.**

a. When does faith stop being easy? When is it hardest for you to have faith?
   Faith stops being easy for me when...

   Faith is hardest for me when...

b. Define faith. (aside from Hebrews 11:1) Break down your definition. Elaborate on it.
   Faith is:

Principle 5 | **The significance of your mentoring ultimately will be measured by the differences the people you mentored make.**

a. What would be your prayer for the most critical difference they will make?

b. How would you measure the success of failure of this difference?

_____

_____

_____

_____

c. Is there one particular difference somebody made in your life that has radically changed you?

_____

_____

_____

_____

_____

Summary Mentoring Definition - Chapter 9

Mentoring is God's limitless grace, infused through your obedience, into the processes of learning and life, affecting the destinies of those you touch.

Give any comments or criticisms you have of the summary definition, above.

_____

_____

_____

_____

_____

_____

_____

_____

Compare your comments or criticisms to those from the Introduction and Chapters 1-8. As before, record strong thoughts or troubling issues you have.

_____

_____

_____

_____

_____

_____

_____

_____

You have completed Chapter 9. Again, consider the questions below. You have done this on two earlier occasions (Introduction and Chapter 5). Do not refer to your earlier answers until you have completed this current set of questions. Then, compare them with the previous lists. See if much has changed and if so, consider why or why not?

List five conditions you would require in order to commit to mentoring someone. How may of these changed since your first list? Briefly write the reasons for the change.

1. _____

_____

_____

2. _____

_____

_____

3. _____

_____

_____

4. _____

_____

_____

5. _____

_____

_____

List five conditions that would stop you from committing to mentoring someone. How may have of these changed since your first list? Briefly write the reasons for the change.

1. _____
   _____
   _____

2. _____
   _____
   _____

3. _____
   _____
   _____

4. _____
   _____
   _____

5. _____
   _____
   _____

Chapter 10 - Just a Little Bit More
Final Thoughts to Consider

Be sure to read Chapter 10 with care. Then, for one final time, reflect on what you have read. Answer the questions provided with each principle below. As always, be as honest and transparent as you can. If possible, discuss your answers in a group.

In the previous nine chapters, the word "love" appeared over two hundred times. God's kind of love (New Testament "agape") is the underlying foundation of biblical mentoring, and my primary motivation for writing "JUST A LITTLE BIT MORE." I have become intimately aware that just a little bit more of God's kind of love every day creates a rock-solid basis for who we are, and what we will do for the Lord. Consider the implications for your life and ministry inherent within the following definition of God's kind of love.

> *God's kind of love, in me, is my intentional, consistent effort to bring as much of God's grace, His presence and His provision to someone, regardless of what it costs me.*

From this definition, we see that God's kind of love is **(1) intentional, (2) consistent, and (3) an effort**. It is deliberate, dependable, ongoing hard work. We see that everything about God's kind of love is intended to deliver God's grace to someone else, through you. Grace is all that is stored up in heaven, just waiting for obedience from a tender heart, so God can dump it all over someone who needs it, when they need it and in the way they need it.

Grace is the purest imitation of Christ and the most powerful demonstration of God that can be experienced.[1] When it comes from you, you become a living display of God's kind of love. It can be explained as a transfer of divine grace. Therefore, if I am going to be successful at loving those I mentor and lead, I am going to have to know, above all things, how to transfer something of God (specifically His love), from within me to a place within someone else.

---

[1] See my definition of grace in "JUST A LITTLE BIT MORE," Chapter 1, Page 20.

We have arrived at the time to put together all nine Summary Definitions of Mentoring. From these, we will extract a final concise definition that sums up the kind of people who willingly offer themselves to the call and purpose of God that identifies them as mentors in the church.

A Final Concise Summary Definition of Mentoring

Mentoring is our intentional, sacrificial imitation and modeling of Christ and His love, in the company of those we are given to care for, lead and develop. We model and teach them what they need to know. We help them practice what they have learned. We inspire them to have the faith to achieve their destinies.

Mentoring, as a process, challenges them to embrace what they have been given, apply it fruitfully to their lives, and develop themselves into all God wants them to be. The goal of successful mentoring is that those it touches shall be forever changed - to the glory and honor of God.

Let's unpack this Final Concise Summary Definition of Mentoring, using the same imagery from Chapter 10 in the book, a puzzle in the shape of a heart. I have listed nine highlights. Take the time to consider each of them.

The Heart of a Mentor

God's Kind of Love

- Mentoring is intentional.
- Mentoring is sacrificial.
- Mentoring is imitation or modeling of Christ.
- Mentoring is taught.
- Mentoring is supervised practice.
- Mentoring is an inspiring impartation of faith.
- Mentoring is a challenge to those we mentor…
  (a) to embrace and become what we have challenged them with.
  (b) to take what they embraced and became so they will bear lasting fruit with it.
- Mentoring is a demonstration of God's kind of love (agape love).
- Mentoring's ultimate purpose is that the people we mentor will touch God and then will touch the world in ways that honor and give glory to Jesus.

As I said in the book, you will notice in the illustration of a heart-shaped puzzle, above, there are blank, unlabeled pieces. The picture is incomplete, because it is your picture. I invite you to look within yourself, to look within your heart. Personalize this puzzle and see what you might add or change. Then add to or revise the bulleted list above. Now, reflect on what your heart's puzzle looks like. Let it speak to you. Listen to it. Learn from it. Draw strength and encouragement from it. Then, go forward, as your life fills in the blanks.

- Mentoring is _____

- Mentoring is _____

- Mentoring is _____

- Mentoring is _____

- Mentoring is _____

- Mentoring is _____

- Mentoring is _____

- Mentoring is _____

- Mentoring is _____

Revise and fill in the familiar lists below, one final time.

List five conditions you would require in order to commit to mentoring someone.

1.

2.

3.

4.

5.

List five conditions that would stop you from committing to mentoring someone

1.

2.

3.

4.

5

Compare your lists, above, with those from Chapters 5 and 9. What have you have discovered about a mentor's heart that will help you clearly understand a great deal about yourself, your call and your potential?

As I wrote in "JUST A LITTLE BIT MORE," consider the following questions one last time.

- Are some of the things you previously thought now becoming less important or perhaps irrelevant? Why?
- Has your vision and understanding of your call to ministry changed progressively as you read through these ten chapters? Do you sense a bigger picture of your life and its purposes now that we have reached the end of the book? What will you do with what you have discovered? How will you do it?
- In what specific ways has your opinion of those you mentor (or will mentor) evolved?

Dr. Bob Abramson

Have other questions arisen? It would be good to seek God and answer them as best you can. Perhaps as you begin to answer them, they will lead you to even more questions. That would be an excellent way to complete your reading of this work.

May God richly bless you and allow you to abundantly bless those you touch for His glory!

Dr. Bob Abramson